T.R.U.E.

e-MOTIONZ

E. Lynn Anderson

DEDICATION

This is dedicated to an individual who had a belief in me when I did not see it for myself.

I would like to say THANK YOU to Traci for having the foresight to entrust in me to birth a desire and dream and executing it towards me. Believing I could nurture this for an outcome of genuine kindness and love for all human beings.

CONTENTS

ACKNOWLEDGMENTS

Thank you LORD and SON of GOD for every piece of my being.

Thank You to my Parents for standing to the side loving and encouraging me enough to allow me to see this dream and desire unfold.

Thank You to EVERY PERSON who said "you could do it".

To You

I had to stop and express to you
some thoughts which crossed my mind
that made me realize just who you are
with a love one-of-a-kind;
First off, you know I care about you
and have done so from our beginning,
but what I failed to acknowledge before
was how much you appease my heart;
Deep down, I've always known that you
were special in unsung ways,
considering the many countless times
you brought joy to all my days;
But suddenly it just hit me that
I discovered in your embrace,
that elusive love I've yearned to find
and could never in life replace;

Yes, now I know just who you are...

a God sent Masterpiece,

whom I'll love and cherish throughout time

until I lay to Rest-In-Peace;

And until that day does come to pass

I'll know in heart and mind,

you gave your all to fill my life

with a love One-of-a-Kind.

E. Lynn Anderson

🦋 Summertime …
MY FAVORITE TIME

Thanksgiving,

Christmas

and Easter Sunday

seasonal holidays come and passed

School is out,

the SUN is shining.

Summertime is here at last…

at the family reunion

excitement is brewing.

The moment is such a thrill,

the music is blaring

and everyone is dancing

while meat sizzles on the grill;

Swimming pools are packed,

the beaches are crowded,

there is much going on in the park.

Vacations out of town

and sold out concerts.

The clubs start jumpin' after dark;

late night cruises on the boulevard

A car show everywhere

The moonlit walks

And heart to heart talks

In a timeless era we share;

The city is buzzing

The brothers are chillin'

While the ladies are dressed to tease,

Then slowly the sun

Begins to fade

Giving way to a cool summer breeze;

It is because of these

And so many other

Special and precious reasons,

That summertime's

My favorite time

    Of all the years' four seasons.

FOND MEMORIES

The fondest memories I cherish

are those that you & I have created together.

They highlight the special & meaningful

moments that we've shared…

The joyful smiles of happiness

when times were at its best.

The caring support & attention

when times were at its worst.

And the tender touches

when we were content with just being near

each other.

What I enjoy most

when I think about the fond memories we've

created,

is knowing that the love & togetherness we

still share now,

will allow us to relive and create more

cherished memories in the years ahead.

If Only This World Were Mine

If only this world were mine

each word I'd sing

in celebration of the joy

to my life it brings;

I'd awaken daily to the sun

and flowers would scent my day,

romantic moonlights would reveal the

 sparkling stars to shine;

I'd never feel the falling rains

no clouds would mar the skies,

and only the tears of happiness

would well within my eyes;

I'd live carefree as the wind

no obstacle would I face,

and all the best life had to offer

I'd embrace;

My every wish would be granted

and every dream in my mind,

as reality would approach

if only this world were mine.

A Special Birthday Poem for You

May joyful smiles and fits of Laughter

Be the highlights of Your Day

As the Best of Good and Wonderful Gifts

Repeatedly Come Your Way;

May Heartwarming Gestures from Family and

Friends

Be Constantly Expressed to You

As all the things you anticipate

Concealed in Wishes Come True;

And in Wishing You a Very

HAPPY BIRTHDAY

Please remember that its' from

My heart I'm praying you will always

Enjoy many more to come

Missing You

The thought of you is always on my mind felt
deeply in my heart

and embodied in my spirit.

No other feelings touch the depths

of my soul like the love and care I feel for
you, and being away from you

is a constant struggle I battle with

to overcome those moments when

I feel as though I'm the

loneliest person in the world.

As distance and circumstances

prevent us from being together now,

I still feel very close to you,

because we are one in many ways.

It makes no difference what

obstacles time places between us

because I'll always be there for you,

and until the day comes when

I can be there with you,

always remember that I'll be right here

spending my days and nights

thinking of you,

loving you,

missing you

and waiting for your return!

WORDS

My words can only say so much

My thoughts give only a clue,

My emotions can be expressed so far

My actions have their limits too;

My dreams only give an inspiration

to the promises of hope perceived,

My destiny remains unknown to the outcome

of my goals yet to be achieved;

So with my heart and soul I've prayed

To our Creator on high above,

To keep my life safe and soundly embrace in

the spirit of true love;

'Cause if it appears I haven't shown enough

through what I've tried to convey,

Please give me time, for it's hard to show my

forever love

in the boundaries of one day.

Just Thought I'd Let You Know

I cannot count the reasons or

describe all the ways I care for you;

For there is no end

to the many beautiful and caring

things you do;

Instead I'll serenade you with

the best of my emotions,

To comfort you through day and night

to show my thanks and devotion;

To toast to you the joys of

Life, Love and Happiness

and celebrate their meanings through

our bond of togetherness;

For it has been you who has instilled

in me a special glow,

That I will cherish for life.

Just thought I'd let you know.

Missing My Family

(Dedicated to Our Soldiers)

Holding all of you close

    in my warmest embrace,

Sharing moments of joy

    nothing could ever replace;

Hearing your sweet laughter

    and seeing your bright smiles,

Missing being there with all of you

    in good times and through storms;

The many gatherings we have in spring,

    the summertime bar-b-cues,

the fall and winter holiday reunions….

    my away from family blues;

But fear not the hour that I endure this

    plight;

For one day we all

    shall again reunite;

Because like all the times before

    this storm too we will weather

for love is the force

    that will keep us together;

So think of me often

    and say prayers for me too,

that God will soon send me

    back home to be with YOU!

A Message from Far-Off

It has been a while now,

my beloved one since

we have written one another a letter.

I trust that all is well with your

family and that you are faring even better.

I was just sitting here

contemplating our futures from a spiritual

view,

when I decided to send this

divinely inspired thought and message to you.

I often say prayers that God will keep you all

in optimum health,

and that daily you will strive to climb higher

within His realm of spiritual wealth;

Through total submission to His will

and the rewards for sacrifice is

His Guarantee;

that we shall find true peace and paradise;

To gain so much for this small price

is not too much of Him to ask,

for of all life's struggles we commit to

master –

there is a less worth of noble task;

That is why my Faith and Works are

sincere and I pray yours are too.

Thinking of You

In You…

I have found the pleasure of viewing
perfection at its best;

You're magnificent and your flawless outer
beauty captures the attention of every eye that
beholds you;

Your charming inner beauty radiates a soulful
glow that always deeply appreciated and
warmly welcomed by everyone in your
presence;

The sparkles of joy that dance in your eyes,
the dazzling brilliance of your heartwarming
smile, the caring gentleness of your gentleness
of tender touch, the sweet melodic tone of
your seductive voice and your graceful stride
and fluid motions, are all evidence that you're
a demonstration of poetry in motion and

among all a burning desire in the hearts of others.

When I think of you, I realize how truly BLESSED I am to be entwined with one of GODs greatest creation in Heart-Mind- and Soul.

Were You Listening?

When I told you that I loved you

Do you believe my words are true?

When I tell how much I need you near

Do you also believe that too?

When I tell you of my desire to bring

Joy to all your days,

Do you believe that I can prove it to you a hundred

different ways?

And when I tell you that you are the one

I just can't live without,

Do you believe that you can trust in me and never

harbor doubt?

I believe we were meant to always be

for no one else could ever do,

and pray with all you heart and mind

you believe as I do too.

You Were on My Mind

Just now I had some thoughts of you

but that is nothing new,

for every moment we spend apart

I think of you then too;

If you'd like to know my thoughts

I'll put it to you like this:

you are the one who fills my life

with untold joys and bliss;

For you constantly fill my being with love and

diligently plant new seeds,

That never fails to grow and fulfill

all my wants and needs;

You stir my soul with warmth and passion

that comforts me in every way;

And give me all the reasons why

in my life I pray you will stay-

So because to me you have proved to be

such a rare and precious find,

I'll always keep you in my close embrace with

warm thoughts in mind…

I am only thinking of you~

E. Lynn Anderson

A Mother Through It All

You have continuously been there for me

from the very beginning,

sharing with me love and care

that comes straight from the heart.

Throughout my young and tender years

you nurtured me with hands

that would evolve the thoughts of a child into

the mindset of a adult.

The paths I chose weren't always

brilliant, for I trudged some long and hard

miles.

But I'll never forget your teachings of how I

could turn my frowns into smiles.

Nor will I erase from memory

the words you'd often said

to help me overcome my fears and

doubts and give me courage to face each day;

'Thank you Mother'

for being there to always see me through for I

have truly been blessed by God with someone

so precious as you.

E. Lynn Anderson

A Special Thought

I'm sending you

my brightest smiles

and warmest hugs to say,

may you find joy

and happiness

in your everyday life.

And with this

pecial Thought of YOU,

I also send a prayer,

that you always be

BLESSED with the best

of Life, Love, and Care.

Continuously I

Your friendship and understanding ways are
always inspirational,

Continuously I experience the true meaning
of love and togetherness…

Your genuine care and
strong and supportive thoughts
have enabled me to achieve goals that
I wouldn't otherwise have been able to reach.

You've provided me with the opportunity to
enjoy many beautiful things in life though
your sincere dedication in helping me see my
dreams manifest themselves into realities.

And you never fail to be there
to soften the hard blows I take;

Your comforting words,
Your reassuring gentle touch,
and ever present smiles.

I relish the quality moments we share
that create feelings of warmth and happiness;

my heart and soul will forever cherish

and its' with you that I'll always be there for
throughout life within our friendship.

With My Love Always ... I DO

With my love always

I walk in this life with you

through whatever comes our way

In times of a crisis,

rest assured that I will be there for you to

share it all;

I will keep myself focused

and pay close attention to our

needs, wants, and desires,

that all requested of me

by you will be fulfilled;

If ever you should find a deficiency

in my support,

please make me aware of it,

that I may do a deeper soul search

to find the answer

appropriately needed

to suffice you.;

You are a true blessing to me

and I devote my life

to showing you just how much

I cherish and appreciate you;

I do this with my love ALWAYS!

Whispering Secrets?

At sunrise of each day

To say how much you're missing me while I

am away.

Do you whisper secrets?

When you're alone in an empty room

Saying how much you're hoping that

I will be home with you soon.

Do you whisper secrets?

To your pillow in a prayer

to say how much with me you need

this lonely night to share.

I miss you very much, sweetheart and

wonder if this is true that just like me,

you also whisper secrets too!

May The Birth of Your Child Bring Much Joy Into Your Life

One of the most wonderful events a person could experience is the elated anticipation of a newborn child.

This celebrated creation of life is very special and it is a true blessing to behold such a cherished moment.

I'm offering you my best wishes on the birth of your child, and wish you much success and happiness in the years of parenting that you face ahead.

As a new parent, your responsibilities in nurturing your child will be many, but I believe with confidence that you will be the most loving and caring parent your child could hope to have, and to be to your child as a parent he or she will always be proud of.

For the # 1 Lady in My Life...

If there were more Mothers

in the world like you

there would be more love around.

Compassion would be

a common sight to see

and care could easily be found.

There would be more appreciation

for the gift of life

that only a Mother could give,

and in the hearts

of all on Earth

the spirit of joy would live.

I'm glad there is you

to make a difference

in that needed special way,

'Cause you're a #1 Mom that I pray God will

bless each and every day.

Father's Day is a Happy Feeling

Any male can donate his seed towards the pro-creation of a child, but it takes an authentic man to stand up and be a Father to that child.

Taking on with enthusiasm the many obligations and responsibilities of nurturing, guiding, and supporting his child with love, truth, knowledge, and wisdom.

The enduring and endless tasks of rearing a child and keeping the family together and securing are just some of the many duties that a true Father will fulfill without questions or procrastination, not only to his children, but also those in his community.

It is for these reasons and so many more that this special tribute of Love, Honor, and Respect.

A Happy Father's Day is one that I have found you to have duly earned.

The Rewarding Joys of Family

Whether it be a large gathering or reunion or

just a small get together,

there is no greater joy for many than spending

quality time with family.

It's a time when that

special, intimate bond of togetherness is

shared by everyone alike,

from the oldest member to the youngest.

It's also a time when the exchanging of

personal greetings, feelings, and ideas

give rise to the spirit and assurance that as one

solid unit they will succeed in life and prosper.

It is those tender moments that are shared

and seasoned with their tears and laughter;

Reminiscing the fond memories of those who

have passed away before them,

and cherishing the presence of those now in
their midst.

To be part of a close knit family'

is surely a blessing that everyone should have
the opportunity to experience in life.

For the rewarding joys of a beautiful bond are
without ending;

This I know and believe in my heart because
you - my family

Are the greatest joys that God has allowed me
to know.

You and I Together

When you and I first fell in love,

it created a feeling between us best described
as

    BEAUTIFUL.

Through the days and moments we spent

together, our love grew strongest and more

meaningful.

Our spirits became more closely entwined,

and our soul manifested as one we became an

extension of the other…

Your smiles were the symbols of my

happiness and your frowns were the pillars of

my sorrows and as yours were mine;

As I look at us;

    TODAY

all we've achieved and struggled against to

overcome;

TOGETHER

I see how over time we've managed to change something that was once hailed beautiful into something that is now best described as;

MAGNIFICENT

Yes, we've come a long way…too far to ever turn back and we've grown too close to ever become as two again.

For in the depths of our love, we've come to realize that life would be nothing in you and I didn't have each other to share it all with.

True Love Takes Time

In the beginning of our relationship
we knew love wouldn't come easy for us.
We experienced joys that we felt would last
forever and frustrations that made us feel like
giving up.
But we never let go because we knew that
love was more than saying the word
   I Love You.
And more than just our immediate feelings
toward each other
over time, our relationship has greatly
matured from our constant dedication in
learning the ways to love
by realizing each other's needs,
mentality, emotions, spirituality, and physically
understanding them, respecting them and
most of all supporting them.

It took a lot of hard work, compromise, and a

relentless pursuit for us to achieve

what we now cherish so deeply.

I'm glad that we took the time to excel where

others so often fail,

for from out of our unending commitment,

we've come to acknowledge that the

most beautiful thing about love is

being blessed with the patience and wisdom

to find and know its true meaning.

My YESTERDAY

Although our relationship is over
a part of me still longs for you;

I never knew that I'd find myself needing you
more;
It's strange how sometimes separation brings
about true admiration

I thought
that what
I had,
once felt,
so strongly
for you

was now locked away deeply in my memory
far from the surface of my emotions;

BUT I was wrong…

Even though I have a new love in my life
now, I still find myself thinking of you very
often in ways that I shouldn't be.

For although I must remain faithful to my
new love, I can't help but wonder if he sees in
my eyes, hear in my voice,
or feels in my touch that my heart
still belongs to you.

FROM ONLY YOU

A smile that speaks HAPPINESS

and a warm and tender KISS.

Moments of

FIERY,

INTIMATE

PASSION

from you these things I miss.

The comfort of a warm EMBRACE

and softly whispered things,

I find myself truly missing

from you, the joys it brings.

A showing of the heart from which

emotions pour out strong like rainbows of

endless love from you, these things I long;

Days and nights filled with adventure and

laughter at every turn,

the contentment of tranquil, quality and time,

from you these things I yearn;

For sweetheart, having you not near makes

me feel down and blue because what I need

most right now can only come from you.

I'm Glad There's You

In loving you

I am fulfilled in my need

of having someone special in my life/

to share my all with

equally and unconditionally/

being loved by you

assures me that my all

is well appreciated,

and I'm comforted in knowing

that all I have to

give and share with you

is never taken advantage of

nor for granted

To realize every reason why

Our love is so special

Is knowing that we have found

In each other

The key to friendship, the secret of happiness, and the foundation of true love.

Exclusively 4 You

Allow me to create for you

a world of love and care,

that through our years ahead will not succumb

to wear or tear;

With determined thoughts for eternal bliss is

how I propose to start;

Asking God to guide me as

I enter your mind and heart;

I will till a garden and sprinkle it with seeds,

from which will grow the fulfillment of all

your wants and needs;

The air you'd breathe would be my ever

burning passionate fire, for in this world I'd

be your one and only true desire;

I'll sow a splendid robe for you to wear

from the comforts of my soul,

then line it with joy and happiness and

warmth that won't grow cold.

Next I would expose you for all on earth to

see this world I built, just for you to last an

eternity;

And if by chance someone should ask,

"However could this be"

I'd tell them that I love you and you mean the

world to me!

- Yesterday's Memory
Today's Reality
Tomorrow's Dream -

-Yesterday-

Is a memory of a day that went too fast

A day in which you gave me

all the reasons

to love you in every perspective

I could,

With my mind, body and soul

throughout the night, you gave my mind

the best dreams I've ever had,

and upon my awakening hour

-Today-

I reminisced and knew

that throughout the day

I would love and care for you

as I did yesterday

adding just a little more,

To let you know how much I appreciate you

when I lay

to sleep tonight,

I will do so loving you

and thinking of you

and saying a prayer that…..

-Tomorrow-

I'll have you here with me

to love and care for

all over again.

"YOUR SMILE"

One of your best qualities that I find so

attractive is your smile

It's comforting, cheerful,

and always a pleasure to see.

Your smile symbolizes the kind of joy

and inner happiness that radiates a soulful

glow that is always appreciated

in the eyes of the beholder.

Few people can smile and truly warm

another's' heart in the special ways yours do,

which makes the rare beauty

of your smile so precious, so alluring,

and so cherish-able.

Me Just Being Me

I must admit to the world

and even you can agree,

there is no greater joy on the planet

earth than me just being me;

First, take a look inside my mind

where it's easy to discern with all the

 knowledge that I now possess;

there's not much more I can learn for

my mental process is infinite.

And not to brag or boast but it's just a

 mere and simple fact

that I know more than most;

Now let's go to my physical being-

I'm tone from head to toe,

and in comparison to anyone else

my body will steal the show;

I work out daily to stay in shape and my

body fat is close to nil;

Others stare and yearn to touch me to

see if I am real;

My attributes and character prove my

potential has been refined,

and no I'm not on an ego trip

It's just that I'm one-of-a-kind;

For I've been blessed with the

aspirations to be all that I can be,

and that's the greatest feeling in the

world…Me just being me!

Beauty Beyond Comparison

Today I saw a flower

glistening with morning dew.

Its colors were bold and vivacious

and it made me think of you.

I reached out and touched its petals

they were so silky soft.

The longer I stood admiring them

the more of you I thought.

You're like the flower that I beheld

gently with my fingertips.

A fine display of nature's beauty;

cause of the smiles of my lips.

But unlike the flower that change of seasons

fades

you continue to blossom year round.

That's why I do all that I can

to preserve in you what I've found.

Asiatic woman of God's creation

you're bountiful yet rare.

And I cherish you for

the soul of beauty beyond compare.

How Sweet It is to be loved by You

The love you share with me is very special

It's warm, comforting, and very attentive.

It's caring, sympathetic, and always respectful.

You give understanding and support of my

needs, as well wants

Without question,

And your dedication of

Seeing the achievements of my desires

Fill me with a strong sense of promise and

hope.

You've always been my friend,

my closest ally and gentle romance.

For so many reasons

Large and small

Your love has been the most wonderful

Joy I've ever known.

You will always be my inspiration

For loving me the way you do…

How sweet it is to be loved by you Heavenly

Father!

Sensuous Dreams of You & Me

Last night I dreamt of you and I

but that was nothing new

for every night you're not with me

 I dream of us then too;

I dreamt that we lay nude in bed

On sweet-smelling silk sheets

Listening to our favorite artists croon

Over smooth and soulful beats;

Champagne and candlelight's help set the

mood

And we play those lovers' games.

The tender sweet kisses and teasing touches

Ignite inner passionate flames

For only a short while the foreplay lasts

When we begin to passionately groove

You stroke my body in every position

And I match you move for move

Then finally that special moment comes when we…

It feels so good we repeat the act two or more times …

We lay exhausted yet satisfied

Each whispering, "I love you"

As we slowly doze off in each other's embrace

The warm morning sun awakens me

yet to another day that I must spend

impatiently waiting for

night fall to come so I can dream of you and I

again!

Untitled

I had to stop and express to you

some thoughts which crossed my mind

those that made me realize just who you are

with a love one-of-a-kind

First off, you know I adore you

and have done so from our start

but what I failed to acknowledge before

was how much you appease my heart

Deep down, I've always known that you

were special in unsung ways,

considering the many countless times

you brought joy to all my days;

But suddenly it just hit me that

I discovered in you embrace

that elusive love I've yearned to find

and could never in life replace

Yes, now I know just who you are…

A God sent Masterpiece,

Whom I'll love an cherish throughout the

ages

Until I lay to rest-in-piece

And , until that day does come to pass

I'll know in my heart and mind

You gave your all to fill my life

With a love one-of-a-kind!

Dear "You" Letter

It's been awhile now, my beloved one

Since we've written each other a letter

I trust that all's well with your family

And that you're faring even better;

I was just sitting here contemplating

Our futures from a spiritual view,

When I decided to send this divinely inspired

Thought and message to you;

I often say prayers that God will keep

You all in optimum health,

And that daily you'd strive to climb higher

within

His realm of spiritual wealth;

Through total submission to His will

The rewards for sacrifice

Is His guarantee that we shall find

True peace and paradise;

To gain so much for this small price is not too

much of Him to ask

For of all life's struggles we commit to master

There's a no more worthy or moral task;

That's why my Faith and Works are sincere

And I pray yours are too

I'm closing now, please take care beloved

And oh yeah, keep in touch!

King or Queen

Allow me to create for you a world of love

and care

that through our years ahead will not succumb

to wear or tear

with determined thoughts for eternal bliss

is how I propose to start asking God to guide

me

as I enter your mind and heart.

I will till a garden and sprinkle it with seeds

from which will grow the fulfillment of all

your wants and needs.

The air you'd breathe would be my ever

burning passionate fire,

for in this world I'd be your one and only true

desire.

I'll sew you a splendid robe to wear from the

comforts of my soul

then line it with joy and happiness and

warmth that won't grow cold...

Next I would expose you for all on earth to

see this world I built,

 just for you to last an eternity

And if by chance someone should ask

"How could this ever be?"

I'll tell them that I loved you and you mean

the world to me!

Because of You

I unremittingly experience the proper

meanings

of love and togetherness.

Your friendship and understanding ways

are always inspirational.

And your genuine care and strong, supportive

thoughts

have enabled me to triumph goals that

without you, I would not have otherwise have

grasped.

You've provided me with the opportunity

to enjoy many beautiful things in life.

Through your sincere dedication in helping

me

See my dreams manifest themselves into

realities

and you never fail to be there

to soften the hard blows I take

with your comforting words,

your reassuring gentleness and ever present

smile.

I relish the quality moments we share

that create feelings of warmth and happiness

that

my heart and soul will forever cherish,

 and it's with you that I will always be there

...

for throughout our life with the upmost of

Love and Friendship.

Special Someone

Tell me sweetheart

   have you ever needed or wanted someone

you could say with confidence and assurance

   was yours and yours alone?

A special someone who would embrace you,

Your dreams and aspirations

Someone who would take time to understand

and care

   about you and all you may feel.

Someone who would be there for you

   no matter how smooth or rough the

journey may be

Someone who would respect and adore you

Just for being you!

A special someone who would love you with

the tenderness touch and strongest

conviction,

be attentive to your every need, want and

desire

And be devoted and exclusive to only YOU!

Well Sweetie,

if you ever had a need for such a special

someone,

then I hope you will take this opportunity

to enter within my world;

where you will find that special someone

who you could with self-assurance, say is

absolutely for you!

THE END

From the Writer:

As I think about how far I've come, I realize it has not been far at all. It's just beginning!
Life is a continuous

lesson,

    teacher,

       mentor,

          friend,

             hardship,

       challenge,

and even an enemy at times. It is a journey which takes time to really embrace and value. Ones' life is viewed within emotions, feelings, understanding, comprehension...........trials and tribulations.

I chose to use LOVE as the foundation of this book of expressions in various display because LOVE is ...Learning Ourselves Vigorously for preparation for Eternity!